**DATE DUE**

| | | | |
|---|---|---|---|
| | | | |
| | | | |
| | | | |
| | | | |
| | | | |
| | | | |
| | | | |
| | | | |
| | | | |
| | | | |
| | | | |
| | | | |
| | | | |

791.6
Pet        Peters, Craig
           Cheerleading stars

# LET'S GO TEAM:
## Cheer, Dance, March

# LET'S GO TEAM:
## Cheer, Dance, March

# CHEERLEADING
# Stars

## Craig Peters

Mason Crest Publishers
Philadelphia

To Alexandra: First a car star, now a cheerleading star—what's next?

Thanks to Valerie Ninemire, cheerleading guide at About.com, for her assistance in assembling material for this book.

Mason Crest Publishers, Inc.
370 Reed Road
Broomall, PA 19008
(866) MCP-BOOK (toll free)
www.masoncrest.com

First printing

1 2 3 4 5 6 7 8 9 10

Library of Congress Cataloging-in-Publication Data

Peters, Craig, 1958-
  Cheerleading stars / Craig Peters.
       v. cm. — (Let's go team—cheer, dance, march)
Includes index.
Contents: What makes a star? — High school stars — Collegiate stars —
All-stars — International stars — Celebrity cheerleaders.
  ISBN 1-59084-533-1
  1. Cheerleading—United States—Juvenile literature. [1.
Cheerleading.]  I. Title. II. Series.
  LB3635 .P434 2003
  791.6'4—dc21

                                                        2002015954


Produced by
Choptank Syndicate and Chestnut Productions
226 South Washington Street
Easton, Maryland  21601

Project Editors  Norman Macht and Mary Hull
Design  Lisa Hochstein
Picture Research  Mary Hull

Printed and bound in the Hashemite Kingdom of Jordan

## OPPOSITE TITLE PAGE

*The University of Kentucky Wildcats have won more UCA National Championships than any other cheerleading squad.*

# Table of Contents

# What Makes a Star?

**B**eing a cheerleader is hard work. There may be times when you feel like quitting, and other times when you feel like cheerleading is the best thing that's ever happened to you. One way to keep track of it all is to keep a diary. You can record what's happening and how you feel about it. When you read back on it later, you may find that your outlook has changed.

*Dear Diary,*

*Hi, it's me. I can't believe I actually made it to cheerleading camp for the first time. The instructors showed*

Cheerleading is about more than winning; it's also about personal growth, physical fitness, and fun.

One way to improve your performance is by attending a cheerleading camp, where you and your squad can receive instruction and learn new skills and techniques.

*our squad the routine we're going to learn, and it looks so awesome! I can't wait to get started! The cafeteria food is totally gross, but I met a lot of kids. One of them, Allie, and I hit it off great. I think our squad is going to be amazing when these two weeks are over. See you later!*

*Dear Diary,*

*The routine we're learning is a lot of hard work. A LOT of hard work. It's unbelievable. I was aching so much last night when I went to sleep. I know it's only been two full days, but there's a part of me that feels like I'm not gonna make it. I'm getting a little discouraged, and I'm starting to feel like this cheerleading camp maybe wasn't such a great idea after all. Well, gotta go. More later . . . if I survive.*

*Dear Diary,*

*Ouch. My knee gave out on me during a stunt today. It was not a pretty sight. Jenny fell on me, and for a second I thought my leg was broken. Good thing the back spotter was right there, or else I might have gotten hurt for real. I felt like everyone was laughing at me. I'm happy to see today end, and I'm gonna sleep well tonight. See you soon.*

*Good news, Diary,*

*It's getting better all the time. I just read my last entry, and I can't believe I sounded that down. Today was great. We worked on stunts all morning, and then on cheers and gymnastics all afternoon. My body's aching, but it's a good ache. We spent some time working on projecting our cheering voices, and I really could hear my own improvement. I can hardly wait for tomorrow— it's performance day!*

*Dear Diary,*

*It was awesome! Our squad won the award for Best Overall Cheer! We were great! We nailed every move, and we were so psyched! I won an award for Most Improved Cheerleader! When I went up to get it, everyone was cheering and yelling, it felt like I was getting an Oscar or a Grammy or something like that! I felt like a total star! Life is good, Diary!*

Behold, the power of cheerleading. One day, it can make you feel like you want to give up. Your body is so sore you think you can't go on anymore. The next day, cheerleading can make you feel like you're on top of the world. You faced a personal challenge, and you did what you had to do to not give up and to be your best. You feel like the biggest star the cheerleading world has ever known.

What is stardom, anyway? The dictionary defines stardom very simply: "The status or position of a star." For many people, a star is somebody who is successful, who has won awards in their chosen profession. People like Diana Ross, The Beach Boys, and Rod Stewart are definitely music stars. Yet none of these stars has ever won a Grammy, the most prestigious award in their chosen profession, the music business.

*The number of squads worldwide continues to grow each year as more athletes, both male and female, are attracted to cheerleading.*

So maybe stardom has less to do with awards than with pure success. Maybe being the best at something is what makes someone a star.

Well, that may be getting closer to an answer, but stardom has to be more than just being the best at what you do. Anna Kournikova has never won a major tennis tournament, but she's one of the sport's biggest stars.

So when all is said and done, it's very hard to say exactly what stardom is. Stardom has to do with success and winning awards, but it also has to do with charisma and public acclaim. When you read interviews with the biggest stars in any field, you see that self-confidence, self-discipline, and determination are qualities they talk about again and again. These are qualities that cheerleading helps develop.

As popular as cheerleading has become, not a lot of well-known stars have emerged. There are celebrities who have been cheerleaders, but there are no stars of

## "STARDOM:" THEY SAID IT

John Wooden, the legendary UCLA basketball coach, said "the main ingredient of stardom is the rest of the team." That certainly applies to cheerleading, where everyone on the squad needs to do their best, and work in conjunction with each other, all for the good of the team.

Milton Berle, one of the biggest early stars in the world of television, once said, "I'd rather be a could-be if I cannot be an are; because a could-be is a maybe who is reaching for a star. I'd rather be a has-been than a might-have-been, by far; for a might have-been has never been, but a has was once an are." Believe it or not, that applies to cheerleading, too. Berle is saying that no matter what your dreams of stardom or success might be, you should go for it with a positive attitude and do your very best. Reach for the star you want.

The legendary guitarist Chet Atkins once said, "A long apprenticeship is the most logical way to success. The only alternative is overnight stardom, but I can't give you a formula for that." Atkins was one of the biggest stars in country music for decades, and his point is a good one. Being a success, being a star, takes a lot of hard work.

It's no different in cheerleading.

cheerleading the way, say, Tony Hawk is a star of skate-boarding or the Williams sisters are stars of tennis.

Even so, there are still cheerleading stars who deserve to be recognized. For example, there are squads on the high school and collegiate levels that seem to be among the national champions year after year, and many other squads whose accomplishments have drawn the attention of the general public. There are also celebrities who were once cheerleaders, who help raise the profile of this ever-growing phenomenon.

As we look at the stars of cheerleading, though, we should point out that there are countless cheerleading squads across the country and around the world. It's impossible to give proper recognition to all the deserving national champions, schools, organizations, gyms, and clubs. Cheerleading is unique because it is growing so fast. According to the National Federation of State High School Associations, competitive cheerleading is the fastest growing girls' sport in the United States. There are so many squads and competitions—72 regionals and nationals in 2002—that it's hard to keep track of them all.

Cheerleading is more than competitions and athletics. The emphasis is on athletic performance, but personal growth and attitude are equally important. These are qualities that can't be measured in trophies or blue ribbons.

In that respect, simply by being a cheerleader, you are as bright a star as anyone you'll read about on the pages that follow.

# High School Stars

**T**here aren't many high school cheerleading squads who have had a book written about them. Then again, there aren't many high school squads like the Greenup County High School cheerleading team of Kentucky.

The book, written by James T. McElroy, is called *We've Got Spirit.* It's a must-read account of a year in the life of one of the best-known high school squads in the country.

Greenup first sent a squad to national competition in 1981. In their first 20 years of competition, they captured nine national titles. The green and gold uniforms of the Greenup cheerleaders are seen annually at the National

*According to the National Federation of State High School Associations, competitive cheerleading is the fastest growing sport among high school girls.*

High School Championships sponsored by the Universal Cheerleaders Association (UCA). Charles Kuralt featured them on his "On The Road" segment for CBS News. The 1997 championship team was even featured in a milk moustache ad.

The Greenup cheerleaders are undoubtedly the best-known high school cheerleading squad in the United States. In Kentucky, they are bona fide celebrities.

Credit for Greenup's success, as *We've Got Spirit* makes clear, has to go to head coach Candy Berry. She cheered for Greenup County's Russell High School in the 1960s. In 1973, she became an assistant coach at Russell High, then moved on to be the head coach at Greenup High. Author James T. McElroy described her success:

> Ever since she led Greenup County High School to its first four national cheerleading championships, in 1981, '82, '83, and '84, Berry has set the example that the rest of the cheerleading world follows. Every competitive cheerleading coach in the country teaches her girls to emulate the cheerleaders from Greenup County, Kentucky. Like [football coach Vince] Lombardi, she's become legendary.

Through the years, Berry has received many lucrative offers to coach college cheerleading programs in Kentucky and elsewhere. She's turned down all the offers and has remained at Greenup, where she receives no pay. She's not really concerned about money, but she is very concerned about the girls in her program.

*The Greenup County High School cheerleaders pose for a group photo. With nine championships to their name, the Greenup squad has become one of the main attractions at the UCA Nationals.*

As *Kentucky Living* wrote in 2000, a lot of the success of Kentucky cheerleading is due to the fact that the cheerleading programs nurture cheerleaders in and out of the classroom. "It's the strength of your program [that makes the difference]," Berry told the magazine.

Hendersonville High School in Hendersonville, Tennessee, has a strong cheerleading program, too. As of 2002, the Commandos had six World Cheerleading Association (WCA) National Championships to their credit. What's even more remarkable is that they won five of those championships in consecutive years, from 1997 through 2001.

*To keep their competitive edge, some high school cheerleading squads practice year round, even during summer vacation.*

"We're known for cleanness, sharpness, and perfection of motions," Coach Betty West told *American Cheerleader* magazine. West has coached the Commandos for 28 years. "We're proud of our enthusiasm, showmanship, and projection, and we stick with a really clean, crisp, winning routine."

The Enterprise High School cheerleading squad in Enterprise, Alabama, has gone where no Alabama high school squad has gone before: 10 state championships,

# BE IT RESOLVED . . .

Tennessee's state representatives were so impressed by the Germantown High School cheerleaders, they passed a resolution honoring them.

"**Whereas,** at the heart of any successful athletic program is a strong cheerleading squad and thus this General Assembly was proud to learn of the exceptional accomplishments of the Germantown High School Varsity Cheerleaders; and

"**Whereas,** the members of the cheerleading squad have maintained an overall grade point average of 3.37 on a 4.0 system; and

"**Whereas,** they have also distinguished themselves as either Regional Champions or Runners-up in the UCA Regional Competition for the last several years; and

"**Whereas,** in 1997–1998, the Germantown High School Cheerleaders were Runners-up in the UCA National Competition; and

"**Whereas,** the Germantown High School Varsity Cheer-leaders are presently the reigning National Champions of the Universal Cheerleaders Association; and

"**Whereas,** because of their many accomplishments, in October 1998, the cheerleaders were invited to Tokyo, Japan where they performed with distinction at the Kumamota Cheerleading Festival and the Japanese National High School Cheerleading Competition; and

"**Whereas,** it is fitting that we specially recognize this exemplary cheerleading squad; now, therefore,

"**Be It Resolved** by the House of Representatives of the 101st general assembly of the state of Tennessee, the senate concurring, that we honor and congratulate the Germantown High School Cheerleaders upon capturing the National Championship of the UCA and wish them well in their future endeavors."

including a run of seven straight varsity titles from 1994 through 2000. Among their many other accomplishments, the squad finished in first place for dance and second place for co-ed cheer at the 2002 CheerSport Nationals.

In Texas, the Victoria High School varsity cheerleaders captured the UCA National Championship in 1999. By doing so, they became the first Texas squad ever to win a national title. Then they repeated the feat with a second national title in 2000. Since then, Victoria High School has been consolidated, and the school name has changed

### KEEP IT REAL, KEEP IT HONEST

Every competition has its own set of rules and guidelines that squads need to follow. One of them may not always be spelled out, because it shouldn't have to be. That's the rule that says all the cheerleaders on a school's squad must be students at the school.

In May 2002, not following that rule cost Florida's Osceola High School squad, the Osceola High Kowboys, its World Cheerleading Association National Co-ed Championship. Adrian Free, a senior at Ocean Springs High in Mississippi, was allowed to join the Osceola team and compete at the WCA championships in December 2001. Osceola coach Kerri Collins said she told Free to enroll at Osceola before the squad competed in the nationals, but he didn't.

It was the first time in the WCA's 17-year history that any squad had been disqualified. The title, and the five-foot trophy that goes with it, was awarded to the runner-up squad, from Bowling Green High School in Bowling Green, Kentucky.

to Victoria Memorial High School. Their new team name is the Vipers, and their colors are black, white, blue, and silver. Their cheerleading ethic, though, remains the same.

"We practice 11 months of the year," Denise Neel, cheerleading director at Victoria Memorial High School, told the *New York Times*. "During the summer, it's three to four hours a day, five days a week. During the school year, it's about two hours a day."

Neel's comments are important ones for cheerleaders everywhere. For every squad like hers that wins a national title as the result of such hard work, there are countless other squads who put in the same kinds of demanding hours just for the love of cheerleading.

# Collegiate Stars

**C**ollege cheerleading has become so big that schools are recruiting cheerleaders in the same way they recruit star football and basketball players. In 2002 there were approximately 225 colleges and junior colleges that offered full or partial cheerleading scholarships. That number is sure to rise as more schools develop cheerleading scholarship programs. Some schools offer stipends of $500. Other schools offer full tuition scholarships. There are as many different types of scholarships offered as there are schools offering them.

College cheerleading is huge because college sports are huge. Successful sports teams can bring a lot of

*The University of Kentucky Wildcats have twelve UCA National College Championships to their name.*

# MALE CHEERLEADERS

Cheerleading began in the late 1800s as an all-male activity. During the 1920s, females were welcomed onto cheering squads. They were generally lighter, and so easier to lift. That allowed the squads to perform more stunts in their routines.

Today, cheerleading is mostly a female activity, but the participation of males is growing. In 2000, *Seventeen* magazine reported that there were more than 600 co-ed college cheerleading teams.

Males are being welcomed back to cheerleading squads because they are stronger than their female counterparts. Their strength allows the squad to perform more impressive stunts.

"For their height and weight, these guys are about twice as strong as the football players," Heidi Robertson, the strength and conditioning coach for the University of Kentucky, told *Seventeen*.

Not only do male cheerleaders bring more strength to a squad, they can also bring more spirit to the school.

"It was definitely different when there were men on the squad," Tamra Tyree, a co-captain of Brown University's cheerleading squad, told the *Brown Daily Herald* in 1996. "The whole environment of the school was different. There was more school spirit."

Even so, male cheerleaders have to work harder to gain respect. Sometimes that respect can come from challenging their football-playing friends to a little one-on-one. University of Kentucky cheerleader Tim Passalacqua told *Seventeen* magazine about a time in high school when he challenged the football team to attend a cheerleading practice. "Only about 1 out of 20 could do some of what we were doing," he said. "After that, the football team respected us."

*The men of the University of Kentucky varsity cheerleading squad have helped make the team one of the most successful in history. Male cheerleaders provide spirit, and their strength makes it possible for the squad to do show-stopping stunts.*

prestige to a college or university. Successful cheerleading squads can do that, too. Appearing in a major competition can bring a lot of positive attention to a squad and a school.

The National Cheerleading Association (NCA) College National Championship competition, for example, is broadcast nationally to millions of homes on the CBS network. Each year nearly 150 colleges and universities compete for top honors at the NCA Nationals. The competition is just as fierce at the Universal Cheerleading

*The University of Kentucky varsity squad won their third back-to-back UCA National College Championship in 2002.*

Association (UCA) Nationals, which are broadcast on the cable sports station, ESPN.

Of course, when the University of Kentucky cheerleading squad is on the floor at a UCA competition, it sometimes seems like everybody else is competing for second place. The Wildcat squad is to cheerleading what Tiger Woods is to golf.

In January 2002, the University of Kentucky squad won an unprecedented 12th UCA National College Cheerleading Championship for NCAA Division 1-A schools. Their first championship was in 1985. That means they've won the title 12 of 18 years, including an astonishing eight years in a row, from 1995 through 2002.

The University of Kentucky squad has built a cheerleading dynasty. They've been featured on high-profile television programs like ABC's *Good Morning America,* the *CBS Morning Show*, and Connie Chung's *Eye To Eye.* They've been profiled in magazines like *Gentlemen's Quarterly, ESPN the Magazine,* and *Seventeen.*

The University of Kentucky was even recognized by President George Bush, who joined Kentucky's Senator Jim Bunning at the White House in March 2002 to praise the cheerleaders. "With eight straight championships the UK cheerleaders have distinguished themselves as one of the elite programs in college athletics today," Senator Bunning said. "The University of Kentucky can be very proud of what these young men and women have accomplished."

"We're trying to be an inspiration to the basketball team," cheer adviser T. Lynn Williamson joked.

The Kentucky cheerleading powerhouse doesn't begin and end with the University of Kentucky. Over at the University of Louisville, the co-ed cheerleading squad has captured eight NCA National titles through 2002.

Morehead State University runs a solid cheerleading program, too. The Morehead co-ed squad has won UCA Division 1 National Championships 12 times in the 15 years between 1988 and 2002. The all-girl varsity squad at Morehead captured the UCA National title four out of five years between 1998 and 2002, missing only in 2000.

In 2000, *Kentucky Living* magazine asked: "How has Kentucky become such a cheerleading powerhouse? It starts, many say, with simple traditional values: family, community, sportsmanship, pride, and the drive to succeed," the magazine wrote. "Add to that each individual cheerleader's desire to be the best, and cheerleading programs that never lose sight of their connection to school and academics."

Of course, Kentucky isn't the only state in the nation with superb collegiate cheerleading. Over in North Carolina, the North Carolina State Wolfpack cheerleaders have won four national titles, most recently in 2001 when their winning two minute and twenty second routine captured the Division I NCA National Cheerleading Championship. As Division I winners, the Wolfpack then faced the winners from all the other NCA divisions. After successfully challenging all of the division winners, the Wolfpack emerged with the highest honor, the Grand National title.

"This was one of our most competitive competitions ever, and North Carolina State had an awesome performance," said Bill Boggs, Vice President of Collegiate Programs for the NCA, about the 2001 competition. "Their score of 9.49 is exceptional and one of the highest scores ever recorded by a cheer squad at NCA Nationals. Their signature 'Wolf Wall' brought the house down."

The University of North Texas (UNT) cheerleading squad has emerged to challenge Kentucky for national honors, winning Division 1-A NCA National College titles in 2000 and 2002. UNT is one of only three

*North Carolina State cheerleaders celebrate a victory for the men's basketball team. The Wolfpack cheerleaders are also competitive cheerleading stars. In 2001 they won the NCA Grand National title.*

Division I-A colleges to have won multiple national championships. Cheerleading has long been popular at UNT, where the first spirit club for athletic teams was formed in 1913.

The University of Oklahoma also has a very strong cheerleading program. Both the co-ed and all-girl squads compete at the NCA Collegiate Cheerleading National

Championships. The co-ed squad won the national championship in 1993, and has placed in the top 10 every year since they began competing in 1991. The Oklahoma all-girl squad was formed in 1997, and has always placed in the top five.

In December 2001, *American Cheerleader* magazine called the cheerleaders of Southern University in Baton Rouge, Louisiana, "the best cheer team you may never

## IT ALL STARTED AT SAM HOUSTON STATE UNIVERSITY

In 1949, a year after he started the National Cheerleaders Association in his hometown of Dallas, Texas, Lawrence R. Herkimer made cheerleading history. He organized the first cheerleader camp in Huntsville, Texas, at Sam Houston State University.

According to the National Cheerleaders Association, "Fifty-two girls attended the seminar, which also included a speech professor to present tips on speaking in front of an audience and an English teacher to aid with cheer rhymes. Neither the English teacher nor the speech teacher impressed the 52 girls, but Herkie did. He used gymnastics and vigorous motions to show them how to stimulate and direct crowd response. The girls were elated. They had experienced a totally innovative phenomenon."

Today, Sam Houston State University spirit programs include dance squads as well as cheering squads. In 1998, the Orange Pride Dance Team finished in first place at the College Dance Team National Championship.

Lawrence Herkimer must be very proud.

have heard of." In 1993, head coach James Smith, himself a former cheerleader, took over the squad. He turned it co-ed and led the squad to three consecutive Black College National titles, from 1998 through 2000. In 2001, the Southern University Jaguars cheerleaders finished 10th at the NCA National College Championships. The following year, they improved that standing to second place.

There are plenty of relatively unknown schools that have excellent cheerleading programs. You probably have never heard of Trinity Valley Community College (TVCC) unless you live in or near Athens, Texas. The Trinity Valley Cardinals cheerleaders compete in the Junior College Division, and can boast seven NCA National Championships through 2002. "They had the most dynamic energy I've ever seen them perform with," TVCC cheerleader coach Shannon Davidson said after her squad's victory. "I'm so proud of them, and so excited for the sophomores on the team. This is back-to-back championships for them."

You've probably never heard of Elmira College, either. It's located in upstate New York, and the school's Soaring Eagles captured an NCA Division II National Championship in 2000. "We overcame so many obstacles on the way to the championship," coach Pat Thompson told *American Cheerleader* magazine. "We had a multitude of injuries and a few girls left after first term. We had to add girls during the second term and quickly bring them up to speed. I think all the negative things bonded us together so closely as a team."

*Morehead State University's co-ed varsity squad has won 12 UCA Division I National Championships. The squad also cheers for the university football and men's basketball teams.*

In 2002 there were more than 600 colleges and universities in the United States with cheerleading programs. The number of college cheerleading programs will undoubtedly increase in the years to come. The number of star squads will also increase. Before long, sports fans nationwide will start to learn what cheerleading fans have known for years: the top stars of college athletics aren't always competing on the football field or the basketball court. Sometimes they can be seen on the sidelines, or the competition floor, or cheering on national television.

# All-Stars

In 2001, *Newsweek* magazine called them "fierce, focused athletes" and "cheerleading's elite." They are cheerleading's all-star teams, and they cheer not for their schools, but for the pure love of cheering. Their numbers are growing larger every day. In the same article, *Newsweek* estimated that approximately 2,500 gyms or clubs in the United States have cheerleading squads. They take the athleticism of cheerleading to the extreme.

*USA Today* reported in 2002 that "the past 10 years has seen the rise of all-star programs, in which kids as young as six begin intensive cheer programs with an emphasis on gymnastics. All-star programs exist apart

*There are approximately 2,500 all-star cheerleading squads sponsored by cheer companies, gyms, or clubs in the United States.*

from schools, like AAU [Association of American Universities] basketball teams: They cheer only to compete."

Here are just a few of the thousands of all-star squads capturing titles and building strong bodies and minds in the world of cheerleading today.

Cheer Athletics Gym in Texas is the largest competitive cheering gym in the United States and a true dynasty in the world of all-star cheerleading. The program began in the spring of 1994 with just two athletes. In the 2001–2002 season, Cheer Athletics teams won an unbelievable 30 national championships, bringing their total number of national team titles to 86. Adding individual and stunt groups to the count pushes their national title total to over 100. In mid-2002, Cheer Athletics boasted, "a Cheer Athletics team has had the highest score of all teams at NCA Nationals each of the last five years. We are the only program to win the prestigious Grand Champion award at All-Star Nationals, winning each of the last three years."

Jim Thorp, president of the American Championships, told *American Cheerleader* magazine in 2001,

What impresses me the most about their [Cheer Athletics'] program is the support crowd they bring with them to competitions. They support not only their teams, but the teams with the best chance to beat them. At one of our competitions, one of their teams came in second, and they don't come in second often. They are used to winning. They were disappointed, but as soon as first place was called, they jumped up and fought through the crowd to congratulate the team that won. That's impressive.

The CYC Raiders of Kenosha, Wisconsin, have an impressive story of a different kind. Formed in 1987 by

## WHAT IT TAKES
## TO BE AN ALL-STAR

The training and commitment needed to be an all-star cheerleader is enormous. Here's the training schedule for Star Athletics, an all-star cheer gym in New Jersey that was formed in 1997. Star Athletics has captured many competition honors, including a World Spirit Federation (WSF) Grand National title in 2001–2002.

**Spring and summer:** Training for the new season begins the second week of June and continues through August. Practices are two and a half hours twice a week, and include warm-ups, strength training, conditioning, gymnastics, tumbling, and stunting. The squad attends at least one camp, a four-day NCA camp.

**Fall:** Practices are three hours each on Tuesdays and Thursdays, with additional practices on Sundays and as needed. Training consists of warm-up, gymnastics, stunting, and development of the routine.

**Winter into spring:** This is competition season, with December to April practices happening three hours a day, four days a week: Tuesday, Thursday, Saturday, and Sunday. Training consists of warm-up, gymnastics, stunting, and work on the squad's routine. The teams attend 10 to 15 competitions, sometimes appearing in two competitions per weekend: one on Saturday, and a second on Sunday. Competitions attended are located not just in the New Jersey area, but also in Texas and Florida.

coach Dorothy Wentland, the CYC all-star cheer and dance squads have no home gym. They practice wherever someone will donate space. School gyms, church halls, and empty warehouses have all hosted CYC training. They proudly boast that they are a team, not a business. "The Raiders parents schlep our mats about from pillar to post, praying for clear skies," says CYC. " 'Covered' conveyance is not always available. The Wisconsin snows have dusted our mats more than once." Determination in the face of the hardships has clearly paid off. The Raiders have scored dozens of honors over the years, most recently including a 2000 world championship, a 2001 national championship, and a first place finish at the 2002 Canadian American Open.

Tennessee's Memphis Elite all-stars are impressive performers, too. Established in the fall of 1992, Memphis Elite now has five competitive dance and cheer squads. Their dance team placed first in their first visit to the Cheer and Dance Alliance (CDA) Nationals during the 1992–93 season. By the 1995–1996 season, Memphis Elite had captured first place in both the dance division and the cheer division at the World Cheerleading Association Nationals. Since then, they've become a fixture at national competitions and a frequent top-five finisher.

Indiana is a state that's well-known for producing excellent basketball teams. They also produce excellent all-star cheerleading squads. One of the best to be found in the Hoosier state is the Premier Stars Elite. Formed in 1995, Premier had its best year yet during the

*One of the youngest all-star competitive cheerleading venues is the Pee Wee Novice Division of the UCA National All-Star Cheerleading Championship. Children in fourth grade or below are eligible to compete in this division.*

2001–2002 season. Premier captured seven first place finishes at the Kentucky State Championships, including the Grand Champion title. They also finished first three times at the U.S. Spirit Championships Nationals in Orlando, Florida, and took six first place finishes at the American Challenge Nationals in Indianapolis, Indiana. Their accomplishments are truly impressive.

*All-star teams are made up of members from various schools. The primary focus of an all-star team is performance and competition.*

Of course, any cheerleader who makes it onto an all-star squad has shown impressive skills and amazing determination. Being on an all-star squad takes tremendous effort.

Anyone who thinks cheerleaders are just a smile and a cheer needs to think again and take a closer look at what all-star cheerleading is all about. All-star cheerleaders are highly skilled athletes who undergo years of rigorous training in order to perform and compete at the top levels. With their dedication and hard work, all-star cheerleaders have helped move competitive cheerleading from the sidelines to the frontlines. These athletes are setting new standards of excellence every day.

# International Stars

The United States may be the birthplace of cheerleading, but the popularity of cheerleading throughout the world is growing every day.

In Great Britain, for example, cheerleading didn't start until 1982. That's when American-style football began to be played there. Since then, cheerleading has grown quickly. According to the British Cheerleading Association (BCA), there were more than 3,500 cheerleaders by mid-2002. In Great Britain, the average age of a cheerleader is 15, and the average cheerleading squad contains 26 cheerleaders. In 2002, new squads were being formed in the United Kingdom at the rate of one every 10 days.

*Japanese cheerleaders perform a traditional dance during a soccer match in Yokohama, Japan, in 2002.*

Star British squads include the Honeybees, who competed at the World Cheerleading Association Championships in Nashville, Tennessee, in 2000. The Honeybees finished in third place in cheer, and took fourth place in dance. The Premier All-Stars competed in Myrtle Beach,

## AMERICAN ENTERTAINERS AND INTERNATIONAL STARS

Since their debut during the 1972–1973 NFL season, the Dallas Cowboys Cheerleaders have become the standard for the blending of showbiz and cheerleading. Their first appearance at SuperBowl X in Miami in 1976 was seen by 75 million television viewers. As the result of that appearance, a phenomenon was born.

In 1978, the Dallas Cowboys Cheerleaders appeared on two network television specials, and in 1979 and 1980 they starred in TV movies.

The Dallas Cowboys Cheerleaders have also worked extensively with the United Service Organization (USO). The squad has made more than 40 worldwide tours of hundreds of American military bases, entertaining millions of military service personnel.

In 1991 the squad received the USO's prestigious "50th Anniversary Award." Six years later, in 1997, their many years of service to the men, women, and families of America's Armed Forces were recognized with the presentation of the USO's first "Spirit of Hope" Award.

As the squad's official Web site reports, "The entire Dallas Cowboys organization is extremely proud of the high regard this nation has for the Cheerleaders and for the distinction they have earned in having performed for more troops overseas than any other entertainer ever."

*The Dallas Cowboys Cheerleaders, shown with Christie Brinkley, perform a Christmas show for U.S. peacekeeping troops stationed in Bosnia.*

South Carolina, at CanAm 2001, and captured second and third place trophies. The Palace Crystals also competed at CanAm 2001, winning second and fourth place trophies. Team Britain is the name of the national all-star squad. In the 2001–2002 season, Team Britain consisted of eight girls and a male coach.

"Cheerleading has taken me to Scotland, Loughborough, Manchester, Belgium, Nashville, and South Carolina to perform and compete," says Bonnie Crow, a member of 2001–2002 Team Britain. "This has been a good opportunity for me to travel and maintain high standards of cheerleading."

"America is definitely the sky for all British cheer-leaders," says Bonnie's Team Britain teammate, Lianne Millard, who cheered for Premier All-Stars.

"The sky" was reached by another star U.K. squad, the Ascension Eagles. They appeared in their first competition in 1997 but did not do well. Then they redoubled their efforts and went on to win top honors in British and European competitions. They were invited to perform in

## HIGH SCHOOL CHEERLEADERS ON MTV

In 2001 the cheerleaders of Paul Lawrence Dunbar High School of Lexington, Kentucky, became international cheerleading stars. It had nothing to do with a competition they had won, though they had been Kentucky state champions many times and had captured a UCA National title in 1995.

The cheerleaders of Dunbar High became stars when they were the subjects of an MTV documentary, *True Life: I'm A Cheerleader.*

"I wanted to capture the athleticism, the drive, and the entire sense that this is not cheerleading as most people remember it," MTV producer Laurie Girion told *American Cheerleader* magazine. Girion, who was a cheerleader herself in high school, also said that "the way Dunbar approaches cheerleading is like going to the Olympics compared to what I used to do."

MTV filmed 190 hours of material, following the squad through tryouts and on to national competition. The final documentary, which lasted 44 minutes, was considered a success by MTV. Their ratings among female teenagers increased 300 percent.

the 1998 Macy's Thanksgiving Day Parade in New York City. The team's success was made even greater by the fact that they're from one of London's roughest neighborhoods. In 1999, the Eagles were profiled in *People* magazine. In the article, one cheerleader's father said this about the team's success: "Our whole lives are full of rubbish, but now our kids are champions."

The BCA proudly states that it's the fastest-growing cheerleading organization in Europe. Even so, England is the second-largest cheerleading community in Europe. The top spot belongs to Germany, which could claim over 4,000 cheerleaders as of early 2002. The ASC Lubeck Cougars are one of Germany's top squads. Founded in 1989, the Cougars were profiled in a 2002 issue of *American Cheerleader.*

Germany was also home to the first World Cheerleading Championship. On May 14 and 15, 2000, the location for this competition, Warner Brothers Movie World outside of Dusseldorf, became the center of the cheerleading world. The National Cheerleaders Association, a division of the Texas-based National Spirit Group, sponsored the championship.

"We've enjoyed huge success at our European Championship," said National Spirit Group's Vice President of Marketing Andy McNeill. "[We] decided it was time to launch a global invitation so that American and Latin American teams could compete there as well. This event is a huge move for us, and the response has been tremendous—a true measure that the sport of cheerleading is as popular and growing as we think it is."

The competition saw 12 countries participating for awards in six divisions. Participating nations included the United States, Germany, Chile, Great Britain, Austria, Slovenia, Italy, Spain, Finland, Switzerland, Sweden, and Denmark.

The United States, represented by Club Cheer of Dallas, took the first world title. Santiago's Chile Cheer took second place, and the Braunshweig Wildcats from Braunshweig, Germany, came in third. Only two-tenths of a point separated the three teams as they headed into the finals.

"It was an unbelievable honor to be asked by the NCA to represent the United States at this event," said Club Cheer Coach Brandi Noble with tears in her eyes. "This is definitely the beginning of something extraordinary, something very big."

Something very big is developing north of the United States, too. Cheerleading in Canada is growing in popularity. Cheerleading developed in Canada as it did in the United States. There were cheerleaders in the late 1800s, and the first female cheerleader joined a squad at the University of Western Ontario in 1939.

Today, the University of Western Ontario Mustang Cheerleaders are one of the country's best-known teams. In 2001 and 2002, the squad captured NCA National College titles. They've also appeared on the silver screen. The squad had a part in the 1994 movie *The Air Up There,* starring Kevin Bacon. Their part in the movie, in which they were known as the St. Joseph Bulls' cheerleaders, was shot in Hamilton, Ontario.

The first Canadian National Cheerleading Champion-ship was held in Toronto, Ontario, in April 2002. The event was hosted by Power Cheerleading Athletics (PCA) in cooperation with the World National Sports Organization (WNSO). More than 50 squads from all over Canada competed for top honors. One of the top stars of the competition, and of Canadian cheerleading today, were the Cheer Force WolfPack, who took first place in the Grand Championships after winning the All-Star/Club category.

Elsewhere in the world, cheerleading continues to grow in popularity. From Mexico to Chile, Malaysia to Japan, Australia to Ireland, and Finland to Russia, the spirit of spirit is taking hold in dozens of countries around the world. In the years to come, national champions will emerge in each country, international champions will be crowned, and many more star squads will be established. Perhaps one day cheerleading will even become part of the Olympic Games.

# Celebrity Cheerleaders

**C**heerleading is an activity that helps focus one's attention toward personal excellence and growth. To be a successful cheerleader, you have to have strong self-confidence and high self-esteem. After all, it takes a lot of belief in yourself and your abilities to stand up in front of a crowd at a game or in front of the judges at a competition. It takes determination and dedication to smile and show positive attitude even on a day when you might not feel like it.

So it comes as no surprise that so many celebrities, particularly in the entertainment field, were once cheerleaders. After all, to be a success as an actor, actress, or

*Long before she appeared in the hit comedy* Bring It On, *Kirsten Dunst was a real-life eighth-grade cheerleader in southern California.*

singer takes that same kind of self-confidence and determination. Standing up and cheering in front of a crowd is similar to standing up and performing in front of an audience. Being judged on your performance at a cheerleading competition is similar to being judged by directors at an acting tryout.

Here are just a few of the many actors, actresses, and musicians who have cheerleading backgrounds.

**ACTORS**

Samuel L. Jackson, perhaps best known as Mace Windu of the *Star Wars* movies, cheered for the Morehouse College Tigers in Atlanta, Georgia. Maybe that's why he's so good with a light saber.

Steve Martin, the star of dozens of movies including *Father of the Bride, L.A. Story,* and *Parenthood,* was a cheerleader. At Garden Grove High School in Garden Grove, California, Martin spread school spirit for the Argonauts.

Jimmy Stewart, who graduated from Princeton University in 1932 and went on to become one of the world's most beloved movie actors, was head cheerleader in his senior year at Princeton. The megaphone he used now belongs to the Jimmy Stewart Museum in Indiana, Pennsylvania.

**ACTRESSES**

Kirstie Alley, who played Rebecca Howe on the TV series *Cheers,* performed cheers for the Buffaloes when she attended Southeast High School in Wichita, Kansas.

*Samuel Jackson, known for his role as Mace Windu in* Star Wars: Episode 1—The Phantom Menace, *was a member of the Morehouse College cheerleading squad.*

Halle Berry, who received plenty of cheers when she won the Best Actress Academy Award for her role in *Monster's Ball,* cheered for the Bearcats at Bedford High School in Bedford, Ohio.

Sandra Bullock, star of such movies as *The Net, 28 Days,* and *Miss Congeniality,* showed some *Speed* on the playing field when she cheered for the Generals at Washington-Lee High School in Arlington, Virginia.

*Sandra Bullock got her start in the limelight when she was a cheerleader at Washington-Lee High School in Arlington, Virginia.*

Katie Couric, the host of the *Today* show, was a popular cheerleader in her hometown of Arlington, Virginia, when she cheered at Williamsburg Junior High and Yorktown High.

Cameron Diaz, the star of dozens of movies, including *Charlie's Angels* and *There's Something About Mary,* felt there was something about cheerleading when she donned the uniform for the Long Beach Polytechnic High School cheer and drill team in Long Beach, California. Yes, this Angel was once a Pollyette.

Beverley Mitchell, who played Lucy Camden in the popular television series *7th Heaven,* cheered for the Eagles at Chaminade High School in West Hills, California.

Kelly Ripa leads morning television audiences through a parade of guests as co-host to Regis Philbin on *Live!*

## BRING IT ON!

Kirsten Dunst may be the most famous celebrity cheerleader, simply because of her starring role in the 2000 hit movie, *Bring It On.* As Torrence "Torr" Shipman, she is the captain of her high school cheerleading squad, the defending national champions. It turns out, though, that the previous captain stole all the squad's moves from another team.

In real life Kirsten, who also starred in *Spider-Man* and *Jumanji,* among many other movies, was an eighth grade cheerleader in southern California.

"I did it for a little bit to kind of fit in more because I was working on my films and I just wanted to be in the in-crowd, kind of more popular," she said. "I had so much fun cheerleading for that year, but then I didn't do it in high school."

Her cheerleading experience paid off when she landed the role in *Bring It On.*

"It definitely helped me a lot with the script, because I knew everything they were talking about. It's so much more involved than what I did as a cheerleader."

*with Regis & Kelly,* but as a cheerleader for Eastern Regional High School in Voorhees, New Jersey, she led crowds in chants for the Vikings.

Meryl Streep, who won Academy Awards for her roles in *Sophie's Choice* and *Kramer vs. Kramer,* won hearts as a varsity cheerleader for Bernards High School in Bernards, New Jersey.

Sela Ward, who starred in the popular television series *Sisters* and *Once and Again,* was a junior varsity and

## HAIL TO THE CHIEF

Cheerleading is not only great preparation for the performing arts, it's also a good background for politics. In fact, at least four U.S. presidents have been cheerleaders: 32nd President Franklin D. Roosevelt, 34th President Dwight D. Eisenhower, 40th President Ronald Reagan, and 43rd President George W. Bush.

"[There is a] connection, the link between a political rally and a pep rally," Jim Nelson of *GQ* magazine once said, talking about the similarities between cheerleading and politics. "[George Bush] must understand that he learned something all those years ago, the important stuff. How to work a crowd, how to exploit a captive audience, how to come off wholesome and energetic and winning."

"He certainly was a leader on campus," said Christopher J. Gurry, a history teacher at Phillips Academy and a classmate of George W. Bush. "He was head cheerleader, which sounds like a joke, but at the time, it was like the head of the Blue Key Society . . . He mobilized the whole school."

varsity cheerleader at the University of Alabama in Tuscaloosa, Alabama.

Reese Witherspoon, star of such popular movies as *Little Nicky* and *Legally Blonde,* was a cheerleader for Montgomery Bell Academy in Nashville, Tennessee. Montgomery Bell is the brother school of Harpeth High, the all-girls school that Reese attended.

Renee Zellweger, who won acclaim for her starring roles in *Nurse Betty* and *Bridget Jones's Diary,* won acclaim in high school as a cheerleader in Katy, Texas.

**MUSICIANS**

Paula Abdul, who appeared in the movie *Coming to America* and had a string of number one pop hits from 1989 through 1991 with songs like "Straight Up," "Forever Your Girl," "Cold Hearted," and "Opposites Attract," was a cheerleader in high school. Abdul later cheered for the Los Angeles Lakers basketball team.

Christina Aguilera, who rose to pop stardom with such songs as "What A Girl Wants" and "Genie in A Bottle," rose to cheerleading stardom in Pittsburgh, Pennsylvania, as a member of the North Allegheny Intermediate High School squad.

Faith Hill, whose albums *Take Me As I Am, It Matters To Me, Faith,* and *Breathe* rocketed her to the top of the country music charts, had faith in cheerleading when she took to the field in Florence, Mississippi, at the McLaurin Attendance Center.

Lauryn Hill, formerly of The Fugees, who embarked on a solo career with an album entitled *The Miseducation*

*Madonna may have picked up some of her dance skills from her cheerleading days at Rochester Adams High School in Rochester Hills, Michigan.*

*of Lauryn Hill,* cheered the Cougars on to victory while getting her education at Columbia High School in Maplewood, New Jersey.

Madonna, who has held the attention of the music world for years with dozens of top hits, held the attention of the crowd as a cheerleader for Rochester Adams High School in Rochester Hills, Michigan.

Natalie Maines, a member of The Dixie Chicks, was a member of the cheerleading squad for O.L. Slaton Junior High School in Lubbock, Texas.

Reba McEntire, one of the biggest country music stars, was a cheerleader for Kiowa High School in Kiowa, Oklahoma. Appropriately, this Oklahoma Girl cheered on a team known as the Cowboys.

Cheerleading no doubt helped these men and women to develop their skills and showcase their talents. Who knows what cheerleading can do for you?

# Internet Resources

**http://cheerleading.about.com/index.htm**
> An About.com directory of hundreds of Web sites, categorized by subject matters like Cheerleading 101, Cheers and Chants, and Fundraising.

**http://www.americancheerleader.com**
> The official Web site of *American Cheerleader* magazine features message boards, chat, and a wide variety of articles available to subscribers.

**http://www.cheerhome.com**
> Created in 1999 for the benefit of cheerleaders and cheerleading coaches, CheerHome.com features news, message boards, articles, and information on cheerleading camps, competitions, and college programs.

**http://www.cheerleading.net**
> Cheerleading.net offers links to hundreds of Web sites for cheerleaders and coaches at all levels. There are also categories for international cheering sites, cheer gyms, fundraising ideas, and more.

**http://www.cheerleading.org.uk**
> The Web site of the British Cheerleading Association has information about championships, camps, and clinics in the United Kingdom. *Cheer Leader,* the journal of the British Cheerleading Association, has many articles online, which will be of interest to readers no matter where they live.

**http://www.dancecheer.net**
> Dancecheer.net is a one-stop "dance and spirit community" for dance team, cheerleading, drill team, color guard, winter guard, mascots, twirling, and performance groups of all ages.

**http://www.nationalspirit.com/home.asp**

The National Spirit Group is the parent company of the National Cheerleaders Association, the group begun in 1948 by Lawrence Herkimer.

**http://www.varsity.com**

Varsity.com offers information on cheerleading and dance. The Universal Cheerleaders Association (UCA), a leader in cheerleading safety and stunt innovation, is also part of Varsity.com. The UCA is one of the largest cheerleading camp providers and competition sponsors in the world.

# Further Reading

Chappell, Linda Rae. *Coaching Cheerleading Successfully.* Champaign, Illinois: Human Kinetics, 1997.

French, Stephanie Breaux. *The Cheerleading Book.* Chicago: Contemporary Books, 1995.

Kuch, K.D. *The Cheerleaders Almanac.* New York: Random House, 1996.

McElroy, James T. *We've Got Spirit: The Life and Times of America's Greatest Cheerleading Team.* New York: Berkley Books, 1999.

Neil, Randy, and Elaine Hart. *The Official Cheerleader's Handbook.* New York: Fireside Books, 1986.

Rusconi, Ellen. *Cheerleading.* Danbury, Connecticut: Children's Press, 2001.

Scott, Kieran. *Ultimate Cheerleading.* New York: Scholastic, Inc. 1998.

# Index

## PICTURE CREDITS

**Front cover:** Tim Jackson Photography   **Back cover:** United Spirit Association (USA) Associated Press/Wide World Photos: 29, 42, 45, 50, 53, 54, 58; Tim Jackson Photography: 6, 11, 14, 18, 22, 32, 34, 39, 40; Greenup County Cheerleaders/Candy Berry: 17; Courtesy of Pat Reece: 25; Courtesy of the United Spirit Association (USA): 8; University of Kentucky/©Joseph Rey Au: 2; University of Kentucky/©David Coyle: 26.

**CRAIG PETERS** has been writing about various aspects of sports and popular culture for more than two decades. His daughter, Alexandra, began her dance and cheerleading training when she was two years old. By the age of 13, Alexandra had competed on several school and recreation teams and been named captain of her middle school cheerleading squad. Craig has long ago given up the idea that this might be a passing fad for his daughter.